W9-CUO-532

ISBN 0-439-20007-5

51295>

EAN

9 780439 200073

"Quote-a-Day" Writing Prompts

180 Thought-Provoking Quotations With Engaging Prompts to Spark Students' Writing Every Day of the School Year

by Jacqueline Sweeney

First Day of School

"Summer goes, summer goes
Like the sand between my toes
When the waves go out.
That's how summer pulls away,
Leaves me standing here today,
Waiting for the school bus."

—Russell Hoban, *Summer Goes*

List 5 to 10 signs that summer is going and fall is beginning.

Eleanor Roosevelt's Birthday 10/11

"All big things in human history have been arrived at slowly and through many compromises."

—Eleanor Roosevelt

Write about a time that you compromised to solve a problem.

Washington Irving's Birthday 4/3

"I fell asleep on the mountain... and everything's changed, and I'm changed..."

—Washington Irving, *Rip Van Winkle*

Imagine that you took a nap and woke up 20 years later. Describe how things may have changed.

"Quote-a-Day" Writing Prompts

180 Thought-Provoking Quotations With Engaging Prompts to Spark Students' Writing— Every Day of the School Year

BY JACQUELINE SWEENEY

SCHOLASTIC
PROFESSIONAL BOOKS

NEW YORK • TORONTO • LONDON • AUCKLAND • SYDNEY
MEXICO CITY • NEW DELHI • HONG KONG • BUENOS AIRES

For Hoyte van der Zee—

my Anam Cara

ACKNOWLEDGMENTS

Thanks to editor-in chief Liza Charlesworth, who brought the idea for a new quotations book to me and encouraged its innovative format.

To Noxon Road School's Linda Olsen—for generously sharing her classroom quotation resources—and to Noxon librarian Catherine Weiss, for the use of her well-stocked reference shelves. Both women aided my research immeasurably.

To Marian Reiner, my agent, who never lets me down.

To my children, Matt and Gabby, who respected my space during the seemingly endless process of rewrites.

To Kama Einhorn, for the contented completion of our first project together.

Cover design by Kelli Thompson
Cover art by Rick Stromoski
Interior design by Kathy Massaro
Interior art by Mona Mark

ISBN 0-439-20007-5
Copyright © 2002 by Jacqueline Sweeney
All rights reserved.
Printed in U.S.A.

1 2 3 4 5 6 7 8 9 10   40   09 08 07 06 05 04 03 02

Contents

Introduction 4

September 5

October 13

November 20

December 28

January 36

February 42

March 49

April 57

May 64

June 72

Introduction

What better way to begin the day than with some wise words? Using quotations in your classroom is a great way to prompt discussion, promote new thinking, and provide a little laughter. Quotes can inspire, inform, provoke, and entertain. By using them as springboards to students' writing, you can help kids reflect on important themes in their lives and connect "big ideas" to their own experience. Quotes are also a wonderful window into other cultures, perspectives, and historical periods.

In this resource, you'll find a quote for every day of the school year. Each quote and activity can easily be copied onto the board or chart paper for the whole class to see. The quotations and companion activities can be used in a variety of ways in your classroom:

- As a way to begin or end the day

- As a springboard to writing workshop or debates

- In connection with your language arts or social studies themes

- As a way to begin discussing a subject relevant to the group at a given time

- As an independent transition activity (the period when a child completes one activity and is waiting for the group to finish)

Quote-a-Day Journals

Many of the activities in this book invite students to make a journal entry. Students might designate one notebook or folder as a "quote journal" in which they can write every day. You can collect the journals weekly and include a written response to students' thoughts.

A Note About Grade Level

Younger students will need a bit more scaffolding than older students. You might modify or add to the prompts, or have a quick discussion beforehand about the writing prompt.

1

"Summer goes, summer goes
Like the sand between my toes
When the waves go out.
That's how summer pulls away,
Leaves me standing here today,
Waiting for the school bus."

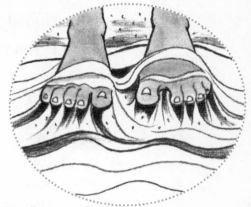

Russell Hoban, "Summer Goes"

ACTIVITY Every season has telltale signs that it is ending. Write two headings at the top of your paper: "Summer Goes" and "Fall Begins." Under each heading, list signs that summer is going and fall is beginning.

"One machine can do the work of 50 ordinary men.
No machine can do the work of one extraordinary man."

Anonymous

2

Labor Day

ACTIVITY Make a list of machines (cash registers, escalators, computers) or machine parts (engines, wheels, pulleys, bolts, levers). Next, write a "word portrait" of someone made out of machine parts! Use your parts list as a reference. For example, your person might have a bolt for a nose, wheels for feet, or a computer for a brain! Use your imagination.

Draw a picture of your machine person to illustrate your written portrait.

3

> Nobody will think you're somebody if you don't think so yourself.

African-American proverb

ACTIVITY Have you ever been the "new kid"? Write a paragraph explaining how you felt on your first day in a new school, or on your very first day of school. Do you think the above quote would have been useful to you?

Back to School

4

> [I'm your teacher]… I work for *you*, for the tilling of your minds and the fruit of your ever-growing souls.

Lois Lowry, Anastasia Krupnik

ACTIVITY Pretend you are the teacher of your class on the first day of school, and write your "lesson plan." List the first five things you would say to your students. Then list the first five things you would do.

5

> I had the feeling that to get into a schoolhouse and study…would be about the same as getting into paradise.

Booker T. Washington
(writing about when he was a slave)

ACTIVITY Who was Booker T. Washington? Look him up in an encyclopedia or on the Web and make a list of his accomplishments. Why was he not allowed to go to school? How did he manage to overcome this problem?

6

> In marble walls as white as milk,
> Lined with skin as soft as silk,
> Within a fountain crystal clear,
> A golden apple doth appear.
> No doors there are to this stronghold,
> Yet thieves break in and steal the gold.

English riddle

ACTIVITY Try to solve the above riddle. Here are some clues: It is a thing you often see in your house. You usually encounter it in the morning but can meet it at other times. It is something you cook. It is kept in the refrigerator. *(Answer: an egg)*

7

End of Revolutionary War

September 3

> We hold these truths to be self-evident, that all men are created equal, that they are endowed by their Creator with certain inalienable Rights, that among these are Life, Liberty and the pursuit of Happiness.

Declaration of Independence

ACTIVITY Look up the word *inalienable* in the dictionary, then choose a partner and discuss what *inalienable rights* means to each of you. Next, work together to create a "List of Inalienable Rights for Kids." Include rights for home and school; for example, the right to be listened to when you have a problem, the right to put ketchup on a hot dog, and so on!

8

National Dog Week

Third Week in September

" [My dog] loved everything about my mother except her high-heeled shoes. When she dressed up, he would bark at her feet, and occasionally one of her shoes would turn up in a neighbor's flowerbed. "

Thomas Wharton, illustrator

ACTIVITY Everyone has a funny pet story, even if he or she is not a pet owner. Think of the funniest true pet story you know and write about it. You might even have a "funny pet story" contest in which everyone shares a story and classmates vote on their favorite at the end!

" Dogs have given up many of their natural ways to cross the boundaries between our species and join our families; for this, each dog deserves lifelong care and protection. "

9

Michael J. Rosen, author

ACTIVITY Write down some "natural ways" you think a dog must give up in order to live peacefully with a family. Next, imagine you are about to leave your family and live with a dog in its environment in the wild. Write down some "natural ways" you would have to give up in order to live peacefully with your canine friend.

**Grandparents'
Day**

September 7

10

66 But I will say that I have
done remarkable for one
of my years, and
experience…
life is what we make it,
always has been, always
will be. 99

Grandma Moses, U.S. painter

ACTIVITY Grandma Moses
didn't begin painting until she was
76 years old, and painted 25
pictures *after* her 100th birthday!
Pretend you are Grandma Moses
at age 100 and write a letter to a
75-year-old sister or brother who
has just said: "I'm too old to try
something new!"

MINI-BIO

Grandma Moses

(1860–1961)

Grandma Moses was born Anna Mary
Robertson and lived for 78 years as a
farmer's wife before being "discovered"
when her paintings were shown at the Museum
of Modern Art in New York City. Grandma
Moses didn't even begin painting until age 76,
when arthritis struck and she could no longer
grasp the small embroidery needles she used to
sew pictures on canvas. Since she had also
become too frail for farm work, she decided to
take up painting! Grandma Moses never had an
art lesson, but was praised for the "freshness,
innocence and humanity" of her work. Her style
was called "American primitive" and reflected
her lifetime of experience on farms in the
Shenandoah Valley of Virginia and upstate New
York. She had her first one-woman show when
she was 80—and never stopped painting until
she died at age 101.

11

66 My grandfather was a giant of a man. When he
walked, the earth shook. When he laughed, the
birds fell out of the trees. His hair caught fire
from the sun. His eyes were patches of sky. 99

Eth Clifford, The Remembering Box

ACTIVITY Describe your grandfather or the grandfather of someone you
know. What does his hair look like? What is his voice like? Does he have a
special habit or favorite activity? Does he have a favorite saying? What kind
of clothes does he wear? And lastly, how do you feel when you're near him?

12

" **If you were born lucky, even your rooster will lay eggs.** "

Russian proverb

ACTIVITY Make up your own funny proverbs about luck. Begin each line with: "If you were born lucky…" For example, "If you were born lucky, even your bull will give milk" or "If you were born lucky, none of your dogs will have fleas."

13

" **Eleven is about the best age for almost anything.** "

Zilpha Kentley Snyder, The Changeling

ACTIVITY Make a *Best Age for…* list in which you decide what different ages are best for. For example, age two is the best age for throwing fits or sucking a thumb; age five is the best age for learning how to tie a shoe. Include your age and the ages 14, 16, 21, 30, 50, 65, and 100.

14

Equal Rights for Women Party Formed

September 20, 1884

" **We hold these truths to be self-evident, that all men and women are created equal.** "

Elizabeth Cady Stanton, U.S. women's rights leader

ACTIVITY The Declaration of Independence begins the same way, except the word *women* isn't in it. Why do you think Elizabeth Cady Stanton added the word *women* to her speech? Do you think modeling her speech after the Declaration of Independence was a good idea? Why or why not?

15

" There are friends, I think, we can't imagine living without. People who are sisters to us, or brothers. "

Julie Reece Deaver, Say Goodnight, Gracie

ACTIVITY Write the names of several people you can't imagine living without across the top of your paper. Under each name, list reasons why these people mean so much to you.

16

" I'm proud of the fact that I never invented weapons to kill. "

Thomas Edison, U.S. inventor

ACTIVITY If you could invent anything in the world to make your life easier, what would it be? A robot boy or girl to do your homework for you? A gadget to help you brush your teeth with no hands? Devise an invention that would make your life easier, draw it, and describe its value and purpose.

17

First American Newspaper

September 25, 1690

" When a dog bites a man that is not news, but when a man bites a dog, that is news. "

Charles A. Dana, "What is News?" in the New York Sun, *1882*

ACTIVITY Look through some newspapers and write down the titles (or headlines) of several articles. Share the most interesting or unusual titles with your class. After sharing everyone's titles, discuss why you do or do not agree with the above quote.

18

**Babe Ruth's
60th Home
Run**

**September 30,
1927**

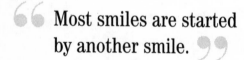

I hit big or I miss big.
I like to live as I am.

Babe Ruth

ACTIVITY Babe Ruth hit his 60th home run in September of 1927. In fact, "The Babe" was famous for doing everything in a big way, from hitting home runs to eating huge meals. Can you think of anyone else who likes to do things in a big way? Describe this person. Be sure to include examples of how he or she thinks and acts "larger than life."

Most smiles are started
by another smile.

Anonymous

19

ACTIVITY Take a walk with a notebook and pen. Walk around your school or playground for six minutes. For the first three minutes, look into the eyes of at least six people, but do not smile at them. Make a note of the number of people who smile at you. For the next three minutes, look into the eyes of at least six people and smile at each of them. Make a note of the number of people who smile back at you. Compare your notes with those of your classmates when you get back.

20

"Fall, leaves, fall; die, flowers, away;
Lengthen night and shorten day;
Every leaf speaks bliss to me
Fluttering from the autumn tree."

Emily Bronte, "Song"

ACTIVITY What makes you know it's October: raking leaves? zipping your jacket? Form small groups and brainstorm all the ways you know it's October—think of weather, clothing, changes in nature, food, sports, special holidays, and so on. Next, draw a leaf pattern on colored paper, cut it out, and write one of your ideas on it. As a group, select places to tape your October leaves, such as windows, doors, above the chalkboard, or on the sides of desks. Or create a tree on a bulletin board!

"I never played on a team until high school [football] gave me a sense of belonging, a focus, and helped build my confidence."

*Howie Long, football player
and sports commentator*

21

**Football
Season**

ACTIVITY Pretend you would like to build someone's confidence by teaching them a new skill: playing a sport, cooking, drawing, and so forth. List five things you would say to this person to help him or her feel confident.

22

"I would rather sit
on a pumpkin,
and have it all to myself,
than to be crowded
on a velvet cushion."

Henry David Thoreau,
American philosopher and poet

ACTIVITY Can you tell by this quote that Thoreau lived alone at Walden Pond, observing and loving nature rather than the company of people? Pretend you are Thoreau writing in your journal about how much you love nature. Use the above quote as your starting sentence, and then continue writing for a few minutes. Don't reread while you're writing; just write whatever comes into your mind!

23

National Children's Day

October 11

"I think I can,
I think I can."

Watty Piper,
The Little Engine That Could

ACTIVITY If a first grader were feeling scared or unsure of herself, what would you say to her? Write down three sayings that might encourage a younger child to feel more confident. The words can be yours or someone else's—any that you find inspiring from a book, a song, or a movie.

24

Eleanor Roosevelt's Birthday

October 11

"All big things in human history
have been arrived at slowly
and through many compromises."

Eleanor Roosevelt

ACTIVITY Look up the meaning of "compromise" and write down its definition. Can you think of a time that you or someone in your family compromised to solve a problem? Can you think of a time when you should have compromised but didn't? Write about one of these times.

> " The basis for world peace is the teaching which runs through almost all the great religions of the world: Love thy neighbor as thyself. "

Eleanor Roosevelt

25

Founding of United Nations

October 24

ACTIVITY Look up *United Nations* in an encyclopedia or on the Web. Why was it founded? Do you think it was a good idea? Do you think Eleanor Roosevelt's idea is in keeping with what the United Nations is trying to do? Explain your answer.

MINI-BIO

Eleanor Roosevelt

(1884–1962)

Eleanor Roosevelt didn't gain the title "the First Lady of the world" for nothing. She spent all of her adult life advocating (speaking out) for human rights, social reform, and peace. Why was she so sensitive to the rights of others? Perhaps because she had lost both her parents and her younger brother by the age of ten, and had experienced her own deep feelings of loss. Whatever the reason, she never wavered from her quest to help the poor and to speak out for their plight. When her husband, Franklin, was elected President of the U.S., she entered politics with him. When he contracted polio and could no longer walk, Eleanor became his "legs," and represented him at speeches and public functions. She had a daily newspaper column and was a regular on the radio, always as an outspoken advocate for the poor and oppressed in America. In later years, she spoke out internationally as well, becoming a delegate to the United Nations. There, she was instrumental in the 1945 adoption of the U.N.'s Declaration of Human Rights.

26

Columbus Day

October 12

" Following the sun,
we left the old world. "

Inscription on one of Christopher Columbus' ships

ACTIVITY Imagine you lived at the time Christopher Columbus sailed from Spain in his journey to discover the New World, when sailors could find their way only by looking at the sun and stars. Pretend you are on the deck of Columbus' ship in the moonlight, watching him gaze at the moon in order to plot the next day's course. Write in your diary about this first night out and how it makes you feel. Be sure to date your entry 1492!

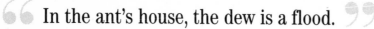

" In the ant's house, the dew is a flood. "

Old saying

27

ACTIVITY Make up your own saying about some tiny creature in nature, such as:

*To a gnat, a sneeze is a hurricane
In a turtle's home, there is no room for chairs.*

Imagine you are a creature experiencing some problem from weather or people, then use your imagination!

28

" No one is lonely while eating spaghetti. "

*Robert Morley,
English actor, author, and humorist*

ACTIVITY What food would *you* most likely eat when you're feeling lonely? Choose a food that is both a comfort and a challenge to eat (a sloppy joe? a hot dog loaded with mustard, ketchup, onions, and cheese? Jell-O?). Next, write a step-by-step set of directions for how to do it.

William Penn's Birthday

October 14

29

"Not to be provoked is best; but if moved, never correct [act] till the fume is spent [until you calm down]…"

William Penn,
Quaker founder of Philadelphia

ACTIVITY The Quakers based their lives on nonviolence as a way of seeking peaceful solutions to problems. Look up the word "provoked" in the dictionary. What do you think William Penn would tell you to do if a person provokes you? Do you think this is good advice? Why or why not? Write down your reasons.

30

"I expect to pass through life but once. If, therefore, there be any kindness I can show, or any good thing I can do to any fellow being, let me do it now, as I shall not pass this way again."

William Penn

ACTIVITY Pretend you are from another planet and have been sent to Earth on a special "kindness mission." You must visit three places and help the people there as well as you can. You have only three days to do it, so you must carefully choose where to visit (any place in your town, in the USA, or in the world). Where would you choose to visit? Explain why you chose each place and list the things you would do there to create kindness.

31

" My greatest fear is being stuck somewhere without a book. "

Patricia MacLachlan, Sarah Plain and Tall

ACTIVITY Pretend you and a friend are stuck in an elevator without a book! Describe three things you might do to pass the time.

" I paint objects as I think them, not as I see them. "

Pablo Picasso

ACTIVITY It's time for a "paint like Picasso" experiment! First look up Pablo Picasso in an encyclopedia or on the Web, or find a book of his art in the library. Look at some of his paintings, especially his portraits of people. Then do the following:

1. Break into groups of two.
2. Look directly into the face of your partner for one whole minute.
3. Close your eyes and *think* of your partner's face.
4. Open your eyes and begin drawing or painting what you saw in your mind, no matter how crazy it appears on the paper.

32

Pablo Picasso's Birthday

October 25

33

Theodore Roosevelt's Birthday

October 27

" Far and away the best prize that life offers is the chance to work hard at work worth doing. "

Theodore Roosevelt, 26th President of the U.S.

ACTIVITY Make a list of work that you are required to do every week (in school and at home). In what ways do you consider it worth doing?

34

" Life is either
a daring adventure
or nothing at all. "

Helen Keller

ACTIVITY How is your life a "daring adventure"? In pairs, make a list of ways you think a kid's life can be daring. Don't forget to consider things like watching scary movies, climbing trees, riding fast on a bike, exploring unknown places, playing a sport, trying a new concept in math, and so on. Then share your list with the class.

35

" It ain't no sin to be glad
you're alive. "

Bruce Springsteen

ACTIVITY Write down five reasons you are glad you're alive on little strips of colored paper. Next, connect all strips together into a paper chain and hang it in the classroom!

36

" If I were smaller than I am;
small as a squirrel…
I'd play baseball with the acorns,
hide and seek among the leaves,
and take long naps stretched out upon
my tree limb balcony. "

Jacqueline Sweeney

ACTIVITY Imagine you are a little animal and it's October. Which animal would you be? What would you do to have fun? Write a little poem or story about yourself as this animal. Be sure to include where you live and a game you'd play. Think *habitat*!

37

"So dull and dark are the November days.
The lazy mist high up the evening curled,
And now the morn quite hides in smoke and haze;
The place we occupy seems all the world."

John Clare, "November"

ACTIVITY Look up the word "occupy" in the dictionary. What place do *you* occupy most in November? Jot down as many facts as you can about November (its weather, holidays, or winter activities).

"A little thought and a little kindness
are often worth more than a great deal
of money."

38

*John Ruskin,
English author and art critic*

ACTIVITY Prepare a "kindness sale." Break into small groups and make posters that list ten possible acts of kindness that someone your age might do. Next, decide what *you* think each kind act should cost! The more outrageous the price, the better you will show how important kind acts are. They are priceless, and yet they are really free! Finally, swap lists and compare prices.

39

Election Day

First Tuesday of November

" The vote is the most powerful instrument ever devised by man for breaking down… the terrible walls which imprison men because they are different from other men. "

Lyndon B. Johnson, 36th President of the U.S.

ACTIVITY Do you think it really matters if a person stays home and does not use his or her right to vote? Write down your answer. Lyndon Johnson thinks voting is a powerful tool. Explain what you think he means in the above quote.

40

" Ladybird! Ladybird! Fly away home, Night is approaching, and sunset is come… "

*Emily Bronte,
Wuthering Heights*

ACTIVITY *Ladybird* is another name for *ladybug*. Look up *ladybug* in an encyclopedia or on the Web. Can you find any clues about why the ladybug is called "lady"? If not, take a guess.

41

Veteran's Day

November 11

" I know war as few other men now living know it, and nothing to me is more revolting. "

Douglas MacArthur, U.S. general

ACTIVITY What is a *veteran*, anyway? Look up the word. Do you know any veterans of war? Make a Veteran's Day card for a veteran.

42

National Creative Child Month

66 I got more thrill out of flying before I had ever been in the air at all— while lying in bed thinking how exciting it would be to fly. 99

Orville Wright, U.S. inventor

ACTIVITY Like many creative people, Orville Wright began inventing in his imagination. Now it's your turn to "invent" a creative kid! Use your imagination and design and describe a creative kid, including his or her activities, favorite foods, abilities, and other qualities. Don't be afraid to describe yourself!

66 Through the use of books I had the whole world at my feet: could travel anywhere, meet anyone, and do anything. 99

Benjamin Carson, surgeon and author

43

National Children's Book Week

Begins November 14

ACTIVITY Have you ever felt you've traveled somewhere in a book? Write about the best place a book ever took you. Next, describe the most interesting person you have ever met in a book.

44

"I think the books I've loved the most are the books that make me experience the entire spectrum of life. They make me laugh and cry and worry. They frighten me."

Katharine Paterson, The Bridge to Terabithia

ACTIVITY Create a "feeling" line for books that you have read—and fill in as many books as you can for each emotion. (The same book can be used more than once.)

happy	sad	afraid	safe	angry	excited	silly

"I found things I could say with color and shapes that I couldn't say in any other way... things I had no words for."

Georgia O'Keeffe, American painter

ACTIVITY Look at some of Georgia O'Keeffe's paintings in an art book or on the Web.

Choose one of her paintings that you like and try to imitate its style using crayons, colored pencils, markers, or paints. Try to paint the way you think she was feeling, letting your crayon or paintbrush go beyond words. Don't try to be perfect—be yourself and have fun!

45

Georgia O'Keeffe's Birthday

November 15

46

"If you want to be loved, be lovable."

Ovid, Roman poet (43 B.C.–A.D. 18)

ACTIVITY Choose three people you care a lot about. Draw the shape of a heart and write the person's name on the top of his or her drawing. Fill the heart with the things that make them happy or feel more loved. For example, in your mom's heart you might write: "picking up my socks," "going out to dinner," "any song by Elvis," and so on.

47

National Education Week

November 16

> More people have to start spending as much time in the library as they do on the basketball court… I think it would make a more basic and long-lasting change in the way things are done.

Kareem Abdul-Jabbar, former professional basketball player

ACTIVITY Think of yourself as an educator. Now brainstorm a list of things someone your age might do to help educate others; for example, being patient and polite can teach a younger brother or sister to be polite, but it can remind someone older as well. As you brainstorm ideas, consider your words, your actions, and how you might set an example at home, at school, and in public.

48

> Nonviolence is the answer… Man must evolve for all human conflict a method which rejects revenge, aggression and retaliation. The foundation for such a method is love.

Martin Luther King Jr. (upon accepting the Nobel Peace Prize in 1964)

ACTIVITY Make a "Stop the Violence" poster using a graphic organizer. Put the word *violence* in the center of a circle. Write six words that mean the opposite and can STOP violence in smaller circles and connect them to the center.

Color the center circle red and the outer circles "peaceful" colors of your choice.

49

> I get by with a little help from my friends.

John Lennon, musician

ACTIVITY Make a list of things your friends do to help you "get by." Next to this list write things you do to help your friends get by. Break into groups and share your lists with each other.

50

Thanksgiving

66 The art of thanksgiving is thanksliving. 99

Wilferd A. Peterson

ACTIVITY Hey, this guy made up a new word! Think about the word *thanksliving*. What do you think it means? Now it's your turn to make up your own compound words using the words *thanks-* and *grateful-* as root words. Write as many words as you can to celebrate your thankfulness for all the good things you experience each day. For example:

thanksturkey   gratefulkid   gratefulpotatoes
thanksfamily   gratefulbrother   gratefulday

66 Bad is never good until worse happens. 99

Danish proverb

51

ACTIVITY Have you ever had a day where nothing went right? Think of an experience that has happened to you or to someone you know that started out bad and then kept getting worse. Number each of the events as you write the details of your experience, then share the results with a friend and console each other!

52

66 It is not enough to have a good mind.
The main thing is to use it well. 99

*Rene Descartes,
French philosopher and mathematician*

ACTIVITY Name three ways you have used your mind well this week. Remember, using your mind well means thinking a task through carefully, whether it's the best way to set the table or where to find Hawaii on the globe.

53

"I am especially glad
of the divine gift of laughter;
it has made the world human and lovable,
despite all its pain and wrong."

W.E.B. Du Bois, educator and author

ACTIVITY It's time for a "Laugh Contest"! Break into groups of three and brainstorm a situation or experience that made one of you laugh really hard. Choose one person to write the situation down and another to either read or perform it for the class. The third person should create and draw a "laugh graph" on the board that goes from zero to ten. After each team performs, take a class vote on which number their laughter achieves on the graph, and mark it accordingly.

"My recipe for success is hard work, patience,
honesty, and total commitment."

54

Dave Thomas, founder of Wendy's

ACTIVITY What is your recipe for success? Write it out as if it were a real recipe. First make a list of at least five ingredients, then write instructions for *when* and *how* to put these ingredients together. Then give your recipe a title. You can be very specific in your choice of subject and title, for example: How to Succeed on a Math Test.

FROM THE KITCHEN OF KARA
SUCCESS CAKE
patience
inspiration
support
confidence
honesty

55

" I am a writer perhaps *because*
I am not a talker. "

Gwendolyn Brooks, poet

ACTIVITY Are you a writer or a talker? Write a short biography about yourself using the following model for a title:

the
_____
(your name)   (writer/talker)

56

" One misty, moisty morning,
When cloudy was the weather,
There I met an old man
Clothed all in leather.
He began to compliment
And I began to grin,
"How-do-you-do,"
And "how-do-you-do,"
And "how-do-you-do, again!" "

Old nursery rhyme

ACTIVITY Pretend you have been contacted by a publisher to write a nursery rhyme for an upcoming book of weather poems for young children. Create a nursery rhyme about any type of weather you choose. Include what time of day your weather occurs, for example: "One thundery blundery night…" or "One sizzly-pizzly morning…" Use your imagination and have fun!

57

> The north wind doth blow
> And we shall have snow,
> And what will the dormouse do then, poor thing?
> Roll'd up like a ball,
> In his nest snug and small,
> He'll sleep till warm weather comes in, poor thing!

Anonymous

ACTIVITY Winter weather causes changes in nature. Some animals stay in cold climates all year and others leave for warmer places. (Some people do the same thing!)

Choose three different animals and describe how each prepares for winter. Then describe the changes that winter brings for you.

58

Deaf Heritage Week

1st Week of December

> You would think the accident would have narrowed my world, limited me. It did the opposite. I started to pay attention to the world instead of taking it for granted.

King Jordan (the first deaf president of Gallaudet University, the only U.S. college for people who are hearing-impaired)

ACTIVITY If you were suddenly to lose your hearing, what things do you think you'd miss hearing the most? Make a list.

59

60

I know I have a first-rate mind, but that's no source of pride to me. Intelligent people are a dime a dozen. But I am proud of having character.

Henry Kissinger,
President Nixon's Secretary of State

ACTIVITY What do you think Mr. Kissinger means by *character*? Look up this word in the dictionary, then make your own list of things someone your age can do to show he or she has character.

I'm just an average citizen. Many black people were arrested for defying the bus laws. They prepared the way.

Rosa Parks

ACTIVITY Read about Rosa Parks in an encyclopedia or on the Web. Do you think she acted like an "average citizen"? Explain your answer.

61

Greatness is a zigzag streak of lightning in the brain.

Herbert Asquith,
Prime Minister of England (1908–1916)

ACTIVITY Brainstorm a list of famous or "great" people you know. Draw and cut out six zigzag streaks of lightning from construction paper. Fill in one name and one accomplishment or quality on each streak of lightning. After sharing what's written on each lightning streak with the class, tape each streak on the wall or bulletin board.

62

Maya Angelou

(1928–PRESENT)

" Music was my refuge. I could crawl into the space between the notes and curl my back to loneliness. "

Maya Angelou, poet

ACTIVITY What does the word "refuge" mean? Look it up if you don't know. What is your refuge? How often do you go there? Write about how your refuge makes you feel.

At the age of eight, Maya Angelou suffered a severe life trauma and as a result she stopped speaking. She did not speak again for several years, but while she was mute, she wrote. And wrote…and wrote! She also found great comfort in music. One day, a kind and sensitive teacher reached out to her, and soon she began to speak again. And she's been speaking ever since! Now Maya is known as Dr. Angelou and is well known all over the world as a poet, historian, educator, best-selling author, actress, playwright, civil-rights activist, producer, and director. She also has a lifetime position as Professor of American Studies at Wake Forest University. She speaks on college campuses everywhere in a manner that seems part dance, part song. And she always captures her audience with the almost magical quality of her voice.

63

Wolfgang Amadeus Mozart's Birthday

December 5

" Mozart is sunshine. "

*Anton Dvorak,
Czechoslovakian composer*

ACTIVITY Have you ever felt this way about someone who makes music? Choose some musical people or groups and write similar sentences. For example, *Beethoven is thunder* or *Britney Spears is a rainbow.*

**Emily Dickinson's
Birthday**

December 10

64

66 If I can stop one heart
from breaking, I shall
not live in vain. 99

Emily Dickinson

ACTIVITY On the top left side
of your paper write the heading:
HOW A HEART IS BROKEN.
On the top right side of your paper
write: HOW A HEART IS
MENDED.

Down the left margin, make a list
of at least six people of *different* ages
starting with the age of a baby and
ending with the age of an old
person. Under the proper headings
write how you think each person's
heart might be broken and how it
might be fixed.

65

66 I never saw a moor,
I never saw the sea;
Yet know I how the heather looks,
And what a wave must be. 99

Emily Dickinson

ACTIVITY Do you actually have to
see something to know what it looks
like? Do you have to *touch* something
to know what it feels like? Beethoven
wrote and conducted his last musical
composition *after* he'd become totally
deaf! Choose a few things you've never
experienced by seeing, touching, or
hearing them, such as an erupting
volcano in Hawaii or a black bear's
claws, and write how you imagine it
would be to experience each one.

66

" That's the way the cookie crumbles. "

" That's the way the ball bounces. "

" That's the way the mop flops. "

American maxims

ACTIVITY Look up the word *maxim* and write out its definition. What do you think these three maxims are trying to tell us? Make up a maxim of your own to say the same thing. For example: "That's the way the worm wiggles" or "That's the way the pudding plops." Write as many as you can!

" This is the most magnificent movement of all!…This destruction of the tea is so bold, so daring, so firm…and it must have so important consequences…that I… consider it as an "epocha" [super moment] in history! "

John Adams,
diary entry about the Boston Tea Party

67

The Boston Tea Party

December 16, 1773

ACTIVITY You can feel John Adams' excitement about watching history being made when he saw the colonists dump all that English tea in Boston Harbor in 1773. Imagine you just saw an important historical moment happen before your eyes (choose an experience that excites you). Pretend you are now at home writing the details in your diary. Be sure to write about it as if you were really there, and make us feel your excitement!

Wright Brothers' First Flight

December 17

68

66 Wilbur and Orville believed that their mechanical aptitude came from their mother...who enjoyed working with her hands. 99

Russell Freedman,
The Wright Brothers

ACTIVITY What abilities do you have? List at least two of your talents or abilities. Then imagine what these abilities might allow you to achieve in the future—and think BIG! For instance, if you draw well, you might become a famous painter, or the director of the Metropolitan Museum of Art in New York City.

13th Amendment— Slavery Abolished

December 18

69

66 Whenever I hear anyone arguing for slavery, I feel a strong impulse to see it tried on him personally. 99

Abraham Lincoln, 16th U.S. President

ACTIVITY Look up the word *abolitionist.* In 1865, the 13th amendment to the U.S. Constitution was ratified (voted into law) to abolish (get rid of) slavery. Can you see how the word *abolish* is related to *abolitionist?* If you were an abolitionist in 1865, write three things you would like to say to someone who was still a slave. Then write three things you would like to say to someone who wanted to continue owning slaves.

70

66 So please, oh *please*, we beg, we pray,
Go throw your TV set away,
And in its place you can install
A lovely bookshelf on the wall. 99

Roald Dahl, Charlie and the Chocolate Factory

ACTIVITY How long do you think you could live without television? If you were told that all TVs would be turned off tomorrow for a year, what is the first thing you would do to pass the time instead? What is the second thing you would do?

71

> I am light as a feather, I am as happy
> as an angel, I am as merry as a schoolboy….
> A happy New Year to all the world!

*Scrooge (after realizing he wasn't dead)
in Charles Dickens' A Christmas Carol*

ACTIVITY If you had a chance to take a tour of your life's important moments or events from the past, would there be anything you'd like to change? Make a list (think of moments when you said things in anger or acted in a way you now regret) and write it down.

72

> What we have to do…is find a way to celebrate our diversity and debate our differences.

Hillary Rodham Clinton

ACTIVITY Look up the word *diversity* in the dictionary, then consider how many holidays and customs help us celebrate the diversity among people and cultures in a wonderful way. Often this includes the handing down of stories, beliefs, and customs from generation to generation. What is your favorite holiday or custom? Do you have any special traditions that you celebrate with your family or friends? Write about them.

73

> It seems that, although languages and customs are different in various parts of the world, there are no differences at all in our hearts.

Mitsumas Anno, author

ACTIVITY Choose a character you like from a book or movie who *seems* very different from you on the outside but *is* like you on the inside (feelings). Make a "same and different" Venn diagram! Fill in ways each of you is different, such as: girl, boy, speaks English, speaks Spanish, and so on. Then, in the overlapping part of the circles, fill in ways each of you is the same, such as: watches out for little sister, lives in an apartment building, and so on. When you have finished comparing the two, decide if you agree with the quote.

74

" A friend is a present you give to yourself. "

Robert Louis Stevenson

ACTIVITY Who is your best friend? Brainstorm a list of sentences that describe your friend's best qualities, such as: "He always listens to me when I have a problem" or "She never forgets my birthday." Now draw a picture of your friend. Next, use these "friend" sentences to make a border around the picture. You might write each sentence in a different color for added pizzazz!

75

" It's tremendously important to have good goals. An aim in life is the only fortune worth finding. "

Jacqueline Kennedy Onassis

ACTIVITY Make a list of your goals for the coming year. Write as many goals as you can think of. Then share some of the results with the class.

76

" A wise old owl sat in an oak.
The more he heard, the less he spoke;
The less he spoke, the more he heard.
Why aren't we all like that wise old bird? "

Nursery rhyme

ACTIVITY What do you think this quote is trying to tell us? Imagine the three quietest people you know before you write down your thoughts.

77

66 **Winter Wise**

Walk fast in snow, in frost walk slow,
And still as you go tread on your toe;
When frost and snow are both together,
Sit by the fire, and spare shoe leather. 99

Traditional

ACTIVITY What do you do when it snows? Do you stay inside? Do you go outside as soon as possible? Make a list of cold weather rules (from your own point of view) for January snow days. Begin the first three rules with *Always* and the next three rules with *Never.* Then start again: three rules with *Always,* three rules with *Never.* Keep following this pattern until you run out of rules! Then come up with a title, such as "Chris's Rules" or "Snow Days According to Vince."

66 Snowy, Flowy, Blowy
Showery, Flowery, Bowery
Hoppy, Croppy, Droppy
Breezy, Sneezy, Freezy 99

78

Anonymous, "The Twelve Months"

ACTIVITY Why do you think the title of this poem is "The Twelve Months"? List the words from the poem one by one in a column down the left side of your paper. Decide which month goes with which word and write it next to that word. Then read the whole list out loud as if it were a poem. Or, make up your own list of words for the 12 months and arrange them in order on the page.

79

"Good-bye is always hello to something else. Good-bye/hello, good-bye/hello, like the sound of a rocking chair."

George Ella Lyons, Borrowed Children

ACTIVITY Use the following sentence frame to make your own Good-bye/Hello list:

Goodbye (to)	Hello (to)

For example, you might write "Goodbye to nine, Hello to ten" or "Goodbye to Summer, Hello to school," and so on. Write as many as you can!

"Nature has many tricks…but the most tremendous, the most stupefying of all is the passive phase of the White Silence. All movement ceases, the sky clears, the heavens are as brass…and man becomes timid, affrighted [scared] at the sound of his own voice."

Jack London, The White Silence

"We had actual daylight all night long. (This was in June.)…You could stand out in the open at midnight, anywhere on the whole mainland of Alaska, and read a newspaper with ease."

Ernie Pyle, Home Country, 1947

80

Alaska Statehood Day

January 3

ACTIVITY Choose one of these quotes about Alaska and imagine you are in the middle of the experience being described. Make a journal entry as if you are the first person from mainland America ever to be in Alaska and are the only person who can bring the experience alive for the folks back home. It will help if you look up *Alaska* in an encyclopedia or on the Web to learn a few facts about temperature, natural surroundings, animal life, and so on before you begin writing.

81

> My boat is turned up at both ends;
> All storms it meets it weathers.
> On its body you'll find not a single board.
> For it's covered all over with feathers.
> Daily we fill it with rice;
> It's admired by all whom we meet.
> You will find not a crack in my boat,
> But you'll find underneath it two feet.
> What is it?

Chinese riddle

ACTIVITY Have a riddle contest! Break into small groups and choose one person in your group to be the reader. This person will read the riddle one line at a time, with some time between each line for thinking. See which group guesses the riddle first. (*Answer: a duck*)

82

> Money buys everything except love, personality, freedom, immortality [never dying], silence, peace.

Carl Sandburg, "The People, Yes"

ACTIVITY Write in your journal about why you do or do not agree with this idea. Include reasons or examples to back up your opinion.

Carl Sandburg's Birthday

January 6

83

Isaac Newton's Birthday

January 4

> If I have seen farther it is by standing on the shoulders of giants.

Sir Isaac Newton, physicist and mathematician

ACTIVITY Sir Isaac Newton discovered the law of gravitation (gravity) in 1643. To us, Sir Isaac seems like the first man to have thought of such things. How do you think the above quotation disputes this way of thinking? What "giants" do you think Newton is speaking of? Write your opinion in your journal.

84

" Example is not the main thing in influencing others. It is the only thing. "

Albert Schweitzer, physician, philosopher, and music scholar

ACTIVITY Who sets a good example for you? Whom do you set a good example for? Make two lists: **1.** People who set a good example for you (they could be family members, people from school, characters in books, people who are famous, and so on). **2.** People *you* set a good example for (your younger brother or sister, classmates, and so forth).

Martin Luther King Jr.'s Birthday

January 15

85

" I have a dream my four little children will one day live in a nation where they will not be judged by the color of their skin but by the content of their character. "

" If it falls to your lot to be a street sweeper…sweep streets so well that all the host of Heaven and earth will have to pause and say, 'Here lived a great sweeper, who did his job well.' "

Martin Luther King Jr.

ACTIVITY In honor of Martin Luther King's birthday, choose your favorite of the two quotes above and write about it in your journal. Why did you choose this quote? What do you like most about it? Do you think Dr. King wants us to learn something from what he is saying? If so, what?

MINI-BIO

Martin Luther King Jr.

(1929–1968)

On the bus ride home after winning a prize for his speech about the Constitution, young Martin Luther King Jr. and his teacher, Sarah Bradley, were taunted and humiliated because they, as African-Americans, refused to give up their seats to white passengers. King felt betrayed that the Constitution didn't protect people of all races (as his prizewinning speech said it did). "That night will never leave my mind. It was the angriest I have ever been in my life," he wrote later. Rather than lash out, King turned his anger into a mission encouraging nonviolence. He devoted his life to the organization of people working to achieve peace and equality for all races. Using Mohandas Gandhi's model for nonviolent resistance, King never lost his dream of full civil rights for all. He was awarded the Nobel Peace Prize in 1964, the youngest person ever to receive the award.

86

> Home is all the words that call you in for dinner, over to help, into a hug, out of a dream.

Michael J. Rosen, author

ACTIVITY What does the word *home* mean to you? Make a list of everything at home that is important to you. After making your list, create a "home collage" that mixes your words with drawings or pictures cut from magazines.

87

Elementary School Teacher Day

January 16

> For every one of us that succeeds, it's because there's somebody there to show you the way out. The light doesn't always have to be in your family; for me it was teachers and school.

Oprah Winfrey

ACTIVITY Brainstorm ideas for what makes a great teacher. How does this teacher present new ideas? How does he or she help you when you're stuck? How does he or she act when you are sad, angry, frustrated, have a birthday, and so on? And finally, what exactly does this person do to make you feel good about learning and yourself?

88

> Everyone teaches, everyone learns.

Arnold Bennett

ACTIVITY Have you ever thought of yourself as a teacher? Think of ways you have helped others to learn (it might be showing a little sister how to tie her shoes, or explaining how to blow a bubble). Write about the ways you teach others. Don't forget that you teach grown-ups as well as friends your own age. For example, think about the last time you helped an adult on the computer!

89

" YY UR
YY UB
ICUR
YY 4me "

ACTIVITY This kind of riddle has two names: a *droodle* or a *rebus*. See if you can solve it. HINT: The letters translate into words! (*Answer: Too wise you are, Too wise you be, I see you are too wise for me.*)

Benjamin Franklin's Birthday

January 17

90

" Speak not but what may benefit others or yourself. "

" Let all things have their places. "

" Lose no time. Be always employed in something useful. "

Benjamin Franklin,
Poor Richard's Almanack, *1753*

ACTIVITY Which one of Ben's sayings do you agree with the most? Write it down and then give an example from your own experience to back up why you chose it. OPTION: Make up your own saying that's similar to one of Ben's, then share it with the class.

Lewis Carroll's Birthday

January 27

91

" Shall I *never* get any older than I am now? That'll be a comfort, one way—never to be an old woman. "

Alice speaking in Lewis Carroll's
Alice's Adventures in Wonderland

ACTIVITY If you could stay any age that you've already been (including how old you are now), what age would you stay and why? If you could be any age that's older than you are now, what age would you choose to be and why?

92

National Freedom Day

February 1

> Proclaim liberty through all the land unto all the inhabitants thereof.

Written on the Liberty Bell

ACTIVITY What does the word *liberty* mean to you? If you were a bell and could "ring out" any idea you wanted to across America, what words would you ring out? Explain why you chose those words.

93

> Freedom! The word tastes like Christmas when I say it aloud. Like a juicy orange or a cup of sweetened milk.

M.E. Lyons, Letters from a Slave Girl

ACTIVITY What does the word *freedom* taste like to you? If you could make up a sound for *freedom*, what would it be? Write a freedom poem using the following frame:

FREEDOM

Tastes like _____

Sounds like _____

Smells like _____

Looks like _____

Feels like _____

94

Weather Person's Day

February 2

> As a rule man is a fool,
> When it's hot he wants it cool,
> When it's cool he wants it hot,
> Always wanting what is not.

Anonymous

ACTIVITY What is your favorite weather? Give five reasons why you like this particular weather.

> Two wrongs don't make one right.

English proverb

95

ACTIVITY What do you think this proverb means? Can you think of a situation where you've seen this proverb in action? Write about it in your journal.

96

Thomas Edison's Birthday

February 11

> I never did anything worth doing by accident, nor did any of my inventions come by accident; they came from work...there's no substitute for hard work.

Thomas Edison

ACTIVITY Describe one of *your* "hard work moments." It might be a moment in sports, an achievement in school, or an art project. Include the following details as you write about your experience:

1. How you felt before you started
2. How you felt in the middle of the hard work (discouraged? tired?)
3. What made you keep going
4. How you felt after your work was finished

97

**National
Forgiveness
Week**

**Second Week
of February**

" It is by forgiveness that one is forgiven. "

Mother Teresa

ACTIVITY Write about a time you forgave someone, and a time someone forgave you.

" My heart is like a singing bird
    Whose nest is in a watered shoot;
My heart is like an apple-tree
    Whose boughs are bent with thickest fruit. "

Christina Rosetti

98

Valentine's Day

February 14

ACTIVITY It's February and that means valentines! Draw a heart that you can trace and cut out. Cut out as many hearts as you like and write a sentence on each one, using the following frame: "My heart is like a…" Think of lovely things in nature, weather, food, clothes, movies, songs, colors, books, and so on to compare to your heart. After writing a poem on each of your paper hearts, sign them, and give them to friends and family on Valentine's Day.

99

Real love begins when nothing is expected in return.

Antoine de Saint-Exupéry, The Little Prince

ACTIVITY Do you love anyone or anything (a parent, a brother, or a sister, a friend or a pet) so much that you'd do anything for them without expecting anything in return? Explain your answer. Is there anyone in your life who loves you this much? Who is it? Why do you think he or she expects nothing in return?

Presidents' Day

Third Monday in February

100

The happiest moments it [my heart] knows are those in which it is pouring forth its affections to a few esteemed characters.

Thomas Jefferson

ACTIVITY Look up the word *esteemed* in the dictionary. Are there any esteemed characters in your life? Write about one of them. Explain why they mean so much to you.

Marian Anderson's Birthday

February 21

101

A voice like hers comes once in a century.

Arturo Toscanini, symphony conductor, speaking about Marian Anderson, opera singer

ACTIVITY Make a list with the heading ONCE IN A CENTURY, then choose the singer, golfer, football player, dancer, artist, teacher, or friend that you consider so outstanding he or she comes along "once in a century." Add any other categories you can think of to your list.

102

" I just want to make a difference,
however small, in the world. "

Arthur Ashe

ACTIVITY List every person you can think of who has made a difference in the world (think of people in sports, music, science, history, and so on). These people do not have to be famous. Then, write one thing (big or small) you think he or she has done to make a difference in the world.

MINI-BIO

Arthur Ashe

(1943–1993)

The word most often used to describe Arthur Ashe is *outstanding*: outstanding athlete, outstanding parent, outstanding human being. He always wanted to make a positive difference with every aspect of his life, and he did it by personal example. Starting at age 15, when he became the first African American to receive a national ranking of fifth among all U.S. junior tennis players, to becoming the first black member of the U.S. Junior Davis Cup Team (which he won) at age 17, to winning the U.S. Open Singles Championship at 25, Arthur never stopped setting a positive example. He beat Jimmy Connors at Wimbledon in 1975 and later took the World Championship Tennis singles title from Bjorn Borg. He contracted AIDS from a blood transfusion received during heart surgery in 1979, and died from the disease in 1993. He is remembered not only as a trailblazer in sports and civil rights, but as a gentle, forthright human being.

103

"When written in Chinese, the word *crisis* is composed of two characters. One represents danger and the other represents opportunity."

John F. Kennedy

ACTIVITY Think of a problem you have experienced. Which part of it seemed dangerous? Which part offered you an opportunity? Remember, the desire to overcome failure and disappointment has lead many people to achieve great success in later life.

"I think of writing as a way of seeing. It's a way of bringing out the specialness of ordinary things."

Lawrence Yep

104

ACTIVITY Who is your favorite author? Do you think this author has helped you to see or think about things in a new or special way? Write about your favorite author and describe one way he or she has changed your way of *seeing* or thinking about something.

105

" Fame is no good. I can have no peace. "

Muhammad Ali,
former world heavyweight boxing champion

ACTIVITY Lots of people wish they could be famous, but there is good and bad in everything. Imagine you are famous. Can you imagine any reason why this might not be a pleasant experience? Write a story about what it might be like to be famous. Title your story:

_____ **the** _____
(your name)   (Great, Magnificent, and so on)

Include some good things and some bad things about being famous.

" Shang ya!
I want to be your friend
For ever and ever without break or decay.
When the hills are all flat
And the rivers are all dry,
When it lightens and thunders in winter,
When it rains and snows in summer,
When Heaven and Earth mingle—
Not till then will I part from you. "

Anonymous, China, first century

106

**International
Friendship
Week**

**Begins
February 18**

ACTIVITY February celebrates so many important themes: freedom, kindness, forgiveness, love, and friendship. As you can tell by the date of this poem, love and friendship have been around for a long, long time. Write a poem about one of your friends (remember, family members can be considered friends, too!). Begin your poem with "Shang ya!"

107

> My feeling is that there is nothing in life but refraining from hurting others, and comforting those that are sad.

Olive Shreiner, South African novelist

ACTIVITY Look up the word *refraining*. Write down three ways someone your age might *refrain* from hurting others. Next, write about three ways you might comfort someone who is sad.

108

> I know I'll survive. I'm a fighter.

Shirley Chisholm,
first African-American woman elected to Congress
and first woman to run for President of the United States

ACTIVITY There are "good" fights and there are "bad" fights. What kind of fighting do you think Shirley Chisholm is speaking of? Create a "fight" list.

1. On the top left side of your paper, write Bad Fights. Under it, write about as many kinds of bad fighting as you can think of.

2. On the top right side, write Good Fights. Under it, write about as many kinds of good fighting as you can think of.

Look carefully at your two lists. Which contains violent *actions*? Which list do you think solves the most problems?

109

Dr. Seuss's Birthday

March 2

> "So you see," bragged the rabbit, "it's perfectly true
> That my ears are the best, so I'm better than you!"

Dr. Seuss,
Yertle the Turtle and Other Stories

ACTIVITY When you read this, how do you feel about this rabbit? Do you know any people who act like this? How do they make you feel? If one of these people were standing in front of you right now, what would you like to say to him or her?

MINI-BIO

Dr. Seuss (Theodor Geisel)

(1904–1991)

Where did Dr. Seuss get all his interesting, wacky ideas? From zoos, of course, and from doodling a lot. No kidding! His father owned a zoo, and as a child, Dr. Seuss would spend hours drawing the animals (his own way!). Dr. Seuss was a cartoonist, and his doodling led him to make a living doing what he loved. He also believed in hard work. Seuss graduated from Dartmouth College and studied literature at Oxford University. He created cartoons for a leading humor magazine and won an Oscar for his cartoon series *Gerald McBoing-Boing*. Dr. Seuss began writing children's stories in 1937 as his antidote to boredom. Also, he felt a lot of kids weren't reading because many of their books did not inspire them to read. Now, over 200 million children have read his books! He said that "nonsense wakes up the brain cells." But he also used this same "nonsense" to write about important issues like prejudice and protecting the environment. Kids of all ages have been delighting in his books since 1937...and probably always will.

110

Alexander Graham Bell's Birthday

March 3

> The telephone is the most important single technological resource of later life.

Alex Comfort

ACTIVITY Alexander Graham Bell, the inventor of the telephone, would be happy to hear this! Look up the word *technology*. What is your favorite technological resource? Why do you think the telephone is so important to people "of later life," such as a grandparent?

Michelangelo's Birthday

March 17

111

> It is well with me only when I have a chisel in my hand.

Michelangelo, 16th-century sculptor and painter

ACTIVITY Create a "well with me" portrait of your entire family, starting with yourself: "It is well with me when I have a _____ in my hand. It is well with Mom when…" Include all your relatives!

112

> Punctuality is the politeness of kings.

Louis XVIII, King of France

ACTIVITY Look up the word *punctuality* and write out its definition. Do you consider yourself a punctual person? Why or why not? Take a Punctuality Poll of the class to see how many kids are punctual and how many are not.

113

> As I was going to St. Ives
> I met a man with seven wives,
> Each wife had seven sacks,
> Each sack had seven cats,
> Each cat has seven kits.
> Kits, cats, sacks, and wives,
> How many were going to St. Ives?

English riddle

ACTIVITY Read each clue carefully and see if you can solve the following riddle. Clues:

1. The answer is simpler than you might think.
2. You don't need math to solve it.
3. The answer is in the first line.

(Answer: one—myself)

> There's a dear little plant that grows in our isle,
> 'Twas Saint Patrick himself, sure, that set it;—
> And the sun on his labor with pleasure did smile
> And with dew from his eye often wet it.

Andrew Cherry, Irish dramatist (1762–1812)

114

Irish-American Month— St. Patrick's Day

March 17

ACTIVITY This quote comes from the song "Green Little Shamrock," which speaks of the legend surrounding the origin of that three-leafed Irish plant. There's another legend about St. Patrick that says he drove all the snakes from Ireland. Do you think either of these legends is true? Look up the meaning of *legend* before you answer. Can you think of other legends (from any culture)? Choose a legend that interests you and try to tell it to the class as a storyteller would.

115

"But I, being poor, have only my dreams;
I have spread my dreams under your feet;
Tread softly because you tread on my dreams. "

William Butler Yeats, Irish poet

ACTIVITY The Irish are often called "dreamers." Some say it's their dreamy nature that's made them famous for their music and poetry. Do you have any dreams for the future? Here's a way you can have a Dream-Share festival with your class:

1. On a small piece of paper, write about a favorite hope or dream for the future. Do not write your name. You might tell about how you've always wanted to be an astronaut or a famous rock star. Or you might tell about something simple, like hoping your best friend will never move away, or how you want a puppy.

2. Fold up each paper and mix them all up in a hat.

3. Each person draws another's dream and shares it with the class.

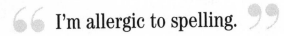

"I'm allergic to spelling. "

116

Barney Saltzberg,
Phoebe and the Spelling Bee

ACTIVITY If Phoebe can make a joke out of having trouble with spelling, so can you—about *anything*! Think about something you might be "allergic" to in a funny way, such as math, going to bed early, and so on. Now make up a funny story about your peculiar allergy. Be sure to include the first time you noticed it, how you reacted (did you sneeze? cough? turn green?), and how you tried to solve the problem. And don't forget to write an interesting title for it that includes your name, such as: Ira and the Math Quiz, or Sarah and Spaghetti Sauce.

117

**National Teacher
Appreciation Day**

March 20

66 Teachers teach more
by what they are
than by what they say. 99

Anonymous

ACTIVITY What do you think
this quote means? Write a letter to
your favorite teacher of all time, being
sure to say thank you for all of his or
her good qualities.

118

66 It is of immense
importance to learn
to laugh at ourselves. 99

*Katherine Mansfield,
writer*

ACTIVITY When is the last time
you laughed at yourself? Did it make
you feel better? Did it make the people
around you feel better? Write about a
"laugh at yourself" experience. It can
reflect a silly or clumsy moment or a
serious one.

119

**Robert Frost's
Birthday**

March 26

66 I always entertain great hopes. 99

Robert Frost

ACTIVITY Look up the word *hope* in the dictionary.
Next, brainstorm a list of your great hopes for your life (now
and in the future). Finally, share the results with the class.

120

Walt Whitman's Birthday

March 26

" Nothing endures [lasts] but personal qualities. "

Walt Whitman

ACTIVITY If *quality* means how good or bad something is, what do you think Walt Whitman means by *personal qualities*? Rate yourself as if you are to be remembered by your personal qualities only. Make a list of your *best* qualities. Include your talents, the ways you show kindness, and so on. Or, make a list of the fine personal qualities of someone in the class. Then share your list without saying the person's name and see if the class can guess who it is.

" As a painter I shall never signify [be known for] anything of importance. I feel it absolutely. "

Vincent van Gogh

121

Vincent van Gogh's Birthday

March 30

ACTIVITY Look up Vincent van Gogh in an encyclopedia or on the Web. Then write a letter to Vincent in which you give him a "pep talk" about himself. Explain which of his paintings you like the best and why. You might even mention how famous he's become and how much his paintings sell for today (millions!).

122

> The question is always the same
> with a dragon: will he talk with you
> or will he eat you?

Arha's prisoner in
The Tombs of Atuan by Ursula Le Guin

ACTIVITY Here's a chance to have fun with creatures! Fill in the blanks with a creature you know about from fantasy books or movies or that you've made up. Then choose an action, such as eating, talking, laughing, and so forth. Create as many "creature questions" as you wish.

The question is always the same with a _____ :

Will he/she _____ **or will he/she** _____ ?

123

> I drew in and colored everything
> across my path.

Ezra Jack Keats, author and illustrator

ACTIVITY Do you have any special interests that you want to do "all the time"? Write about this interest and explain how *you* express it (at home? at school? someplace else?). Later, as a group, make a classroom Special Interest Chart on which everyone writes a sentence or two next to their name, describing the interest that matters most to them.

124

> I like to think in the bath…I'm closed away from
> everything. There is nothing to do but relax.

Eve Bunting, author

ACTIVITY Where do *you* like to think? In a treehouse? In your attic? What do you think about when you're there? Write a story about this place. Call it "My Thinking Place." Include lots of details about this place so that your reader feels like he or she is there, too.

125

" Spring

The fields breathe sweet; the daisies kiss our feet,
…In every street these tunes our ears do greet:
Cuckoo, jug-jug, pu-we, to-witta-woo!
Spring, the sweet spring! "

Thomas Nashe (1567–1601)

ACTIVITY Can you figure out who or what is singing in line 3? Make your own list of sounds that we might hear in spring, and then use these sounds in your own poem about spring. Use this as a starter line: "Here comes spring!"

" Wouldn't it be nice if roses could talk?
I'm sure they could tell us such lovely things. "

126

L.M. Montgomery,
Anne of Green Gables

ACTIVITY Pretend you are a new spring rose. What would you say to people? To bees? To the wind? To the sun? The rain? Write a story about a talking rose. You can write from the "I" point of view, where you are the rose, or you can write about the rose from the observer's point of view where the rose is "he," "she," or "it."

127

Washington Irving's Birthday

....

April 3

66 I fell asleep on the mountain...
and everything's changed, and I'm changed.... 99

Washington Irving, Rip Van Winkle

ACTIVITY Imagine that *you* took a nap under a tree, like Rip Van Winkle did, and woke up 20 years later. Imagine yourself waking up and walking around your neighborhood or into your town. What are the roads and buildings like? Are there still computers or TV? What about clothing styles, food, cars, nature and the environment? Write a story of your experience called

"Rip Van _____."

(your last name)

Booker T. Washington's Birthday

....

April 5

128

66 If you want to lift yourself up,
lift up someone else. 99

Booker T. Washington

ACTIVITY Make a list of uplifting people in your life who have helped you when you felt sad or defeated. Next to each name, write what this person did to lift you up or make you feel better. Next make a list of anyone *you* have "lifted up," and how you did so.

World Health Day

....

April 7

129

66 The first wealth
is health. 99

Ralph Waldo Emerson

ACTIVITY Make a list of ways in which you stay healthy. Include foods, forms of exercise, daily habits, and so on.

130

> " One could get a first-class education from a shelf of books five feet long. "

Charles William Eliot,
former president of Harvard University

ACTIVITY Make a list of the books that have taught *you* something important about life—for example, something about the environment, feelings, a sport, math, poetry, and so on. Then break into small groups for a "book talk," in which you talk about your books with each other.

> " I am the Lorax. I speak for the trees. I speak for the trees, for the trees have no tongues. "

Dr. Seuss, The Lorax

131

Arbor Day

April 10

ACTIVITY Choose your favorite tree (it might be one you climb or sit under to read, or simply one you think is beautiful). Now pretend you are this tree and that you can speak! You might talk about the kid who climbs you every day, or how it feels when the icy wind blows in winter or when a bird makes a nest in your branches in spring.

132

66 April is the cruelest month. 99

T. S. Eliot, poet

ACTIVITY Some people love winter, others don't. Some love springtime, others don't. If you could cut any month out of the calendar, which one would it be? Explain why you'd get rid of that particular month. If you could have any month occur twice, which one would it be? Why?

National Week of the Ocean

April 13

133

66 The voice of the sea speaks to the soul. 99

Kate Chopin

ACTIVITY Write about a time you visited the ocean. What did it sound like? How did it make you feel? If it could talk, what do you think it would say? If you've never visited the ocean, write about a visit to any body of water, such as a pond, a lake, or even a swimming pool!

134

> "There is more treasure in books than in all the pirate's loot on Treasure Island."
>
> *Walt Disney*

ACTIVITY Books are treasures! On a piece of paper, write the titles of your three favorite books and circle each. (Space them out so you'll have room to write around them.) Next, draw five lines from each circle (like spider legs). Attach an empty circle to the end of each leg. Fill in each circle with a "treasure" you found in each book. A treasure might be a feeling that a book gives, a new fact you've learned, a character who seems so real he or she is like a friend, a character you've learned from, and so on. Then take a crayon make each circle a different color.

MINI-BIO

Walt Disney

(1901–1966)

Do you ever wonder who created the first cartoon? You guessed it: Walt Disney. He made it in 1923 and called it *Oswald the Rabbit*. Of course, it was in black and white, as was Walt's first Mickey Mouse cartoon, which hit movie theaters in 1928. There was no television back then, so the only way to see *anything* was in a theater. But Walt didn't stop there. In 1937, he produced the first color cartoon: *Snow White and the Seven Dwarfs*. Then he went on to produce many of your favorites: *Bambi*, *Dumbo*, and *Pinnochio*. Walt Disney received many awards for his pioneering work in films, including more than one Academy Award. You've probably guessed by now that Walter Elias Disney is also the father of Disney World! And the father of Mickey Mouse, Minnie Mouse, Goofy, Donald Duck, Porky Pig....

135

Earth Day

April 22

> The most important thing about Spaceship Earth— an instruction book didn't come with it.

Buckminster Fuller, creator of the geodesic dome

ACTIVITY Imagine you were asked to create an instruction book for Earth for someone from another planet who is about to visit here. Break into groups of two and brainstorm ten do's and ten don'ts for a chapter called "If You Wish to Be Invited Back, You Will…"

> The world is so empty if one thinks only of mountains, rivers and cities; but to know someone here and there who thinks and feels with us, and who, though distant, is close to us in spirit, this makes the earth for us an inhabited garden.

Johann Wolfgang von Goethe, poet

136

ACTIVITY Create your own "garden" that is filled with people who are close to you (old friends, new friends, family members, neighbors, teachers). Draw a flower or plant to stand for each person you wish to live in your garden. Write the person's name on the stem or petals. Surround your "people garden" with mountains, rivers, cities—or whatever else you choose.

137

William Shakespeare's Birthday (and Day of Death!)

April 23

> Which can say more than this rich praise— that you alone are you.

William Shakespeare

ACTIVITY We all have different qualities that make us who we are. What makes you *you*? Write about your qualities: your likes and dislikes, your talents, your favorite animals, books, sports, and clothes.

138

Trouble is a part of your life, and if you don't share it, you don't give the person who loves you a chance to love you enough.

Dinah Shore, singer

ACTIVITY Whom do you go to when you have troubles to share? Write about this person, and explain what he or she says or does to make you feel better. Are there people who come to you when they have troubles? How do you feel when you help them?

139

Good medicine tastes bad...just as good advice hurts your ears.

Yoshiko Uchida,
The Best Bad Thing

ACTIVITY Do you agree or disagree with this quote? Why or why not? Include examples from your own experience to back up how you feel.

140

April Rain Song

Let the rain kiss you.
Let the rain beat upon your head with
 silver liquid drops.
Let the rain sing you a lullaby.
The rain makes still pools on the sidewalk.
The rain makes running pools in the gutter.
The rain plays a little sleep-song on our roof at night.
And I love the rain.

Langston Hughes

ACTIVITY What do you love most about April? Write your own poem praising it, "April _____ Song." Consider starting your poem the same way Langston Hughes started his; for example:

**"Let the baseballs fly in spring.
Let them plop in your glove..."**

141

> I will be the gladdest thing
> Under the sun!
> I will touch a hundred flowers
> And not pick one.

Edna St. Vincent Millay

ACTIVITY Think of good May things: flowers, sunlight, soft breezes. Then begin your own May poem by imitating the first line of this poem. Change the words to suit your own meaning, of course; for example:

"I will be the _____ girl/boy _____ !
I will _____."

142

> I got the blues thinking of the future, so I left off and made some marmalade. It's amazing how it cheers one up to shred oranges or scrub the floor.

D. H. Lawrence, author

ACTIVITY What do you do when you get the blues? Create a "Beat the Blues" poster. As a class, brainstorm as many ways as possible to get rid of sad feelings. Choose the best ideas and write them on brightly colored pieces of paper. Decide together on a picture that gives an uplifting feeling to put in the center of your poster (either drawn, cut from a magazine, or downloaded from the Web). Paste your brightly colored ideas around the central picture. Title your poster in big bright letters, sign your names on the bottom, and hang it in the classroom or in the school hallway to cheer up other friends.

143

Cinco de Mayo

May 5

"It is not just about remembering the Mexican victory over France. It's a day of celebrating who we are! It is a day of pride. It is a day of remembering what my parents gave me and a day to pass those traditions along to my own children. It is a day to say I am proud to be Mexican-American!"

Dorothea Garza

ACTIVITY On the Web, investigate ways to celebrate Cinco de Mayo. Pretend you are having a Cinco de Mayo party and plan three events for it (activities, food, music, special costumes, and so on). Share the results of your research and then together plan a real Cinco de Mayo party for your classroom.

144

National Physical Fitness Month

"I want to be remembered as a person who felt there was no limitation to what the human body and human mind can do."

Carl Lewis, Olympic track star

ACTIVITY Do you think a person needs to be an athlete to keep physically fit? Make a list of activities a person your age might do to keep fit (besides sports, be sure to include activities such as taking out the trash, outdoor games, and so on).

145

"A man should never be ashamed to own that he has been in the wrong, which is but saying...that he is wiser today than yesterday."

*Jonathan Swift,
English satirist (1667–1745)*

ACTIVITY Write about a time when you were wrong about something, and realized it later. Include your reasons for realizing you were wrong or changing your mind, and explain whether you consider yourself a little wiser for making this choice.

146

Rabindranath Tagore's Birthday

May 6

" The butterfly counts not months but moments,
And has time enough. "

Rabindranath Tagore, poet

ACTIVITY What do you think Tagore means by this statement? Look up the life cycle of the butterfly in an encyclopedia or on the Web. Write down how long a butterfly lives, and all things he has time for in his lifespan, then try to answer the question again.

147

" Little Nancy Etticoat, in a white petticoat,
and a red nose.
The longer she stands, the shorter she grows. "

English riddle

ACTIVITY Try to solve this riddle using only one clue at a time.

Clue 1. Nancy, the little girl, is being compared to a thing.

Clue 2. Its nose is not only red but hot.

Clue 3. If the hotness isn't stopped, it ends up as a puddle.

(Answer: a candle)

148

Harry S. Truman's Birthday

May 8

" The buck stops here. "

*a sign on the desk of
Harry Truman, 33rd President of the United States*

ACTIVITY Have you ever heard of "passing the buck?" This refers to people who don't want to take responsibility for their actions, so they "pass the buck" or "the blame" onto someone else for some wrong *they* have done. If you could put a sign on your desk to express how you really feel about life, what would be written on *your* sign? Explain your reasons.

149

" When I give
I give myself. "

Walt Whitman

ACTIVITY Do gifts always have to be given on special holidays or on birthdays? Do they always have to be bought at a store? Think of a time you gave the gift of *yourself* to someone. (Did you take time to read a story to your little sister, or visit your grandmother when you wanted to go out to play instead?) Write about this time and how it made you feel afterward.

Mother's Day
Second Sunday in May

150

" To describe my
mother would be
to write about
a hurricane
in its perfect power. "

Maya Angelou, poet and author

ACTIVITY Describe your mother (or any woman you choose) by comparing her to the following things: **1.** A kind of weather (snow, fog, drizzle, a tornado). **2.** A kind of clothing. **3.** A kind of food. **4.** Something in nature (a leaf, a deer, a red rose). Begin each line with: "My mother is like _____ ." When you're finished, you'll have a Mother's Day poem!

151

" My personal hobbies are reading,
listening to music, and silence. "

Edith Sitwell, poet, novelist, and critic

ACTIVITY Make a list of your hobbies, then share your favorite three with the class.

152

"The old woman I shall become will be quite different from the woman I am now."

George Sand, author

ACTIVITY Have you ever imagined what you will be like when you are old? First, imagine your life from now until then (your profession, your family, your home, your personal qualities). Next, write a detailed description of yourself as an old person. Then, someone other than you can read your "older self-portrait" anonymously and the class can try to guess who each author is.

153

"The best thing to give your enemy is forgiveness…to a friend, your heart… to a father, deference; to your mother, conduct that will make her proud of you…."

John Balfour

ACTIVITY Construct a "Best Thing to Give" chart, and then fill it in with your own choices for people and ideas. Include your teacher, pets, neighbors, and so on:

THE BEST THING TO GIVE

my mom is _____

my dad is _____

my little sister is _____

154

"A weed is a plant whose virtues [good qualities] have not been discovered."

Ralph Waldo Emerson

ACTIVITY Do you know which plants are flowers and which are weeds? The dandelion is considered a weed, but it has a certain beauty many people admire. Look up *weeds* on the Web and make a list of the ones you think have some good qualities!

155

First Woman's Solo Flight Across Atlantic by Amelia Earhart

May 20, 1928

> To want in one's head to do a thing for its own sake; to enjoy doing it;… to concentrate all of one's energies upon it—that is not only the surest guarantee of its success. It is also being true to oneself.
>
> *Amelia Earhart*

ACTIVITY Is there anything in your life (an activity, a sport, playing the piano, dancing) that makes you feel "true to yourself" each time you do it? Write about this experience and describe how it makes you feel.

MINI-BIO

Amelia Earhart

(1898–1937)

As a child, Amelia Earhart hated watching things happen from the sidelines. Once, she built a one-car roller coaster and rode it off her grandmother's shed roof. Earhart also loved the Ferris wheel, and watching daredevil pilots. Finally, after her first ride in an open-cockpit plane, she worked to pay for her flying lessons with Neta Snook, the only woman pilot in America at the time. Amelia Earhart started off on various jobs or careers—nurse's aide to soldiers after World War I, studying to be a doctor at Columbia University, serving as a social worker—but nothing interested her like flying. Even though three women had lost their lives attempting it, she became the first woman to fly across the Atlantic Ocean alone. Earhart also flew alone from Honolulu to the U.S. mainland, and across the country. While attempting a flight around the world, she disappeared. Her words reveal why she might have taken so many chances in the sky: "Nothing on sea or land can be more lovely than the realm of clouds."

156

"The biggest thing in my life is baseball…
I think about baseball a lot. Like most of the time.
I also dream of baseball. Even when I'm awake."

Robert Kimmel Smith, Bobby Baseball

ACTIVITY What is the "biggest thing in your life" right now? Do you think about it all the time? Do you dream about it? Write a story about the biggest thing in your life. Be sure to include the details of when and how you began doing this "thing" and how it makes you feel inside when you do it well. Then give your story an interesting title, such as Dancing Erika, Soccer Sam, or Rhoda the Reader.

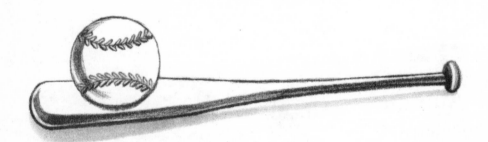

"I have cherished the ideal of a democratic and free society…in which persons live together in harmony…It is an ideal for which I am prepared to die."

Nelson Mandela,
South African President

ACTIVITY Nelson Mandela spent 20 years in prison because of his belief in South African freedom from apartheid. Look up the word *apartheid* in an encyclopedia or on the Web. Explain why you think Nelson Mandela was prepared to die to end apartheid.

157

**Freedom Day
in Africa**

May 25

**Nelson
Mandela's
Birthday**

May 10

158

John F. Kennedy's Birthday

....

May 25

> To be courageous…requires no exceptional qualifications, no magic formula…. It is an opportunity that sooner or later is presented to us all.

John F. Kennedy

ACTIVITY In your own words, write what *courage* means. When is the last time you or someone you know was courageous? Were you scared but did it anyway? Explain what happened.

159

> Failure always makes me try harder the next time.

Michael Jordan,
I Can't Accept Not Trying

ACTIVITY In your journal, describe a time when you or someone you know failed at something, but kept trying until success happened. Include how it made you feel when success finally occurred.

160

> When I think of your good heart, you no longer seem to me so ugly.

Clifton Johnson,
in a retelling of Beauty and the Beast

ACTIVITY Have you ever met anyone who is so good-hearted (friendly, kind, funny, and so forth) that they seem beautiful, even when they might not be beautiful or handsome on the outside? Write about this person and explain what he or she says and does to make him/her seem so beautiful.

161

"I will write you a letter, June day. Dear June Fifth, you're all in green, so many kinds and all one green, tree shadows on grass blades…. The air fills up with motor mower sounds. The cat walks up the drive…"

James Schuyler

ACTIVITY Brainstorm a list of June experiences that matter to you. Perhaps it's playing baseball, enjoying the warm weather, having school about to end, or going to the beach. Next, write your own letter to June using your list of ideas.

"Do what we can, summer will have its flies."

Ralph Waldo Emerson

162

ACTIVITY Make a summer poster of all the things you think summer will have in store for you. First, brainstorm a list of five to ten good things (like barbeques and swimming), as well as a list of five to ten not-so-good things (like mosquitoes and poison ivy). Then, decorate your poster in any way you wish—being sure to include lots of summer colors!

163

Martha Washington's Birthday

June 2

> " The greater part of our happiness or misery depends on our dispositions and not on our circumstances. "

Martha Washington,
the first First Lady of the United States

ACTIVITY What kind of *disposition* do you have (look up disposition if you aren't sure what it means)? Think of a time when you or someone you know was cheerful in the midst of a problem or a difficult situation (a parent, friend, coach, or teacher). Describe what happened. Now describe what might have happened or how you or others might feel if this person had acted in a cranky or impatient way.

> " Give a man a fish and you feed him for a day. Teach a man to fish and you feed him for a lifetime. "

Chinese proverb

164

ACTIVITY Break into groups and discuss the meaning of this poem. Hint: If you tie your little brother's shoes every day you help him for a day. If you teach him how to tie his shoes, you teach him for a lifetime. Brainstorm three more examples to show the meaning of this proverb and share them with the class.

165

Pet Appreciation Week

Second Week of June

" There's just something in me that doesn't trust a cat. "

Stuart Little, a mouse, in Stuart Little *by E. B. White*

ACTIVITY All animals have enemies (other animals, people, bad weather). Work in small groups and design a "Protect Your Pet" poster:

1. Choose a pet (yours or someone else's).

2. Brainstorm six to ten enemies this pet might have (other animals? people? traffic? weather?). Try to imagine yourself as this critter when you brainstorm.

3. Next to each pet enemy, write one or two ways you might keep the pet safe.

4. Arrange your information in a fun way on a poster; for example, you mightdraw (or paste) a small picture of your pet in the middle and write ideas around it, or you might draw a large picture and put ideas inside it!

166

" Let your conscience be your guide. "

Jiminy Cricket

ACTIVITY Look up the word *conscience*. When was the last time your conscience was *your* guide? Write about it in your journal. Be sure to describe what happened and how it made you feel to do the right thing.

167

" You face south, it faces north. You appear sad, it is also sad. You appear glad, it is also glad. "

Chinese riddle, 18th century

ACTIVITY Break into teams and see who can solve this riddle the fastest.

Clue 1. It is something you use every day.

Clue 2. You use it in more places than just your house.

Clue 3. It lets you know if you have spinach in your teeth.

(Answer: a mirror)

168

National Flag Week

· · · · · · · · ·

Begins June 7

" If in a foreign land, the flag is companionship, and country itself, with all its endearments. "

Charles Sumner

ACTIVITY A flag means a lot to a country's citizens (think about the winners of each Olympic event and how they wear their flags on their uniforms!). This week, let's honor other peoples' flags. Write the names of 10 to15 nations and put them in a hat. Break into small groups. Each group draws one country's name, then goes to an encyclopedia or the Web and finds a picture of this country's flag. Draw it on paper or the object of your choice—a piece of cloth, a stone, a poster—then display it in honor of National Flag Week. Or, display your drawing (without the name showing), and have the class guess which country it represents.

" The greatest thrill in the world is to end the game with a home run and watch everybody else walk off the field while you're running the bases on air. "

Al Rosen

169

National Little League Baseball Week

· · · · · · · · ·

Begins June 9

ACTIVITY What would be the greatest thrill in the world for you? (It doesn't have to be about baseball; it could be about anything.) After you've decided and written down a few things about it, have a Greatest Thrill Debate, in which everyone has three minutes to stand up and describe a powerful moment from his or her own life. Remember, a powerful moment could be the way you felt when you first saw your new baby sister, or when you first rode a two-wheeler.

170

> " Reading is a creative activity.
> You have to visualize the characters,
> you have to hear what their voices
> sound like. "

Madeleine L'Engle

ACTIVITY Choose a paragraph from your favorite book in which a character talks about something that matters to you. Practice reading this speech out loud as if you were this person. If you can, make up a voice that you think fits this person. Then share your "speech" with the class.

MINI-BIO

Madeleine L'Engle

(1918–PRESENT)

Most people consider Madeleine L'Engle a children's writer, but she doesn't see it that way. "I just write," she explains. In fact, her Newberry Award-winning book *A Wrinkle in Time* was rejected by many publishers at first because they couldn't figure out if was for children or adults. Madeleine knows that some books she writes are more complicated than others, and she hopes adults will enjoy them, too. She had a lot of hard times at first, when no one would publish her work, but she stuck with her personal vision, and eventually became the inspiring author she is today. How does she do this over and over again? She writes every morning whether she feels like it or not, and definitely considers sitting down and getting started the hardest part. She also believes in rewriting—a lot! Madeleine reads, reads, reads, anything and everything, from books about physics to mysteries. But most of all, she appreciates readers, and not just those who read *her* books. Madeleine believes if it weren't for readers, there would be no exchange of ideas or creativity. And she feels that is what writing (and her life) is all about.

171

Ben Franklin's Kite Experiment

June 15

❝ Actions speak louder than words. ❞

Benjamin Franklin

ACTIVITY What do you think Ben Franklin meant by this? Do you think he would have discovered electricity if he just sat around and talked about it? Describe an action you have taken in your life that shows results and makes you proud.

❝ We always have enough to be happy
if we are enjoying what we do have—
and not worrying about what we don't have. ❞

Ken Keyes Jr.

172

ACTIVITY Brainstorm a "Happiness List"—writing down all the things in your life that bring you happiness, little things as well as big things. For example, you might include "My birthday" as a big thing on your list, but you might also include "The smell of chocolate-chip cookies baking" as a small thing. Remember, both are important!

173

Father's Day

Third Sunday of June

❝ Davy Crockett's father could grin a hailstorm into sunshine, and could look the sun square in the face without sneezing. ❞

Walter Blair, Tall Tale America

ACTIVITY Write a tall tale about your father (or someone else's father). HINT: Think of Paul Bunyon—he was bigger than life! Begin by describing your dad from head to toe. For example: "His eyes are big as two blue ponds. When he breathes, swirling winds stir the sea." Then you might describe a dad adventure— such as playing golf or sailing a boat. Any "dad moment" is fine, even brushing his teeth. It's up to you to make it bigger than life!

174

"You never know what is enough
unless you know what is more than enough. "

William Blake,
English poet (1757–1827)

ACTIVITY   Think about the times you experienced "too
much" of something: for example, too much popcorn at the
movies, or too much sun on your first day at the beach. Write
about one of these experiences (you might title it "Too Much
_____ !") Include the details of how good the experience
felt before it became "too much" and how it made you feel later
to have experienced "too much"! End with a word of advice to
anyone else who might become tempted to do the same thing.

"To be nobody but yourself...means to fight
the hardest battle which any human being
can fight, and never stop fighting. "

175

e.e. cummings, poet

ACTIVITY   Have you ever been in a situation where you
didn't think you acted like yourself? It might have been a time
when other people pressured you to do something you
thought was wrong, or a time when you were afraid to
disagree. Now's your chance to "rewrite" a piece of your life
about a time when you did not act like yourself! Rewrite the
event the way you would like it to be today.

176

We should all be concerned about the future because we will have to spend the rest of our lives there.

Charles F. Kettering,
engineer and inventor (1876–1958)

ACTIVITY How does this statement apply to someone your age? Think about it and then write your reaction to this quotation in your journal. Include ways *you* might show concern for the future—for you and your family!

177

Native American Citizenship Day

June 15

In 1492 there were six million native people residing in what is now the U.S. They spoke 2000 languages, and had been part of thriving civilizations long before the coming of Columbus.

Wilma Mankiller,
Chief of the Cherokee Nation of Oklahoma, 1994

ACTIVITY In 1924, Native Americans were made citizens of their own country! If you could rewrite history in regard to the treatment of Native Americans, list some things that you would change.

178

You must have a garden. Wherever you are.

Patricia MacLachlan, Sarah, Plain and Tall

ACTIVITY It's June—time for gardens! Some people hate gardening while others love it. Which one are you? Explain why or why you *do* or *do not* agree with the above quotation. Give all your "nitty-gritty" reasons why you do or do not like gardens or gardening.

179

" I don't know what our destiny will be; but one thing I know; the only ones among you who will be really happy are those who will have sought and found how to serve. "

Dr. Albert Schweitzer,
physician, philosopher, music scholar

ACTIVITY Look up the word "destiny" in the dictionary. In your journal, describe someone whose *destiny* has brought him or her happiness through helping others. This person need not be famous.

" Night is come,
     Owls are out;
Beetles hum
     Round about.

Children snore
     Safe in bed;
Nothing more
     Need be said. "

Henry Newbolt, 1862–1938

180

Endings

ACTIVITY It's the end of the school year. Write your own poem describing how it feels. Start with your surroundings, for example:

**"Books are closed,
     Desks scrubbed..."**

Your poem doesn't have to rhyme, but it should talk about what you see and how you feel. Choose what matters to you. It can be serious or silly!